PEOPLE of ACTION

Stories of Men and Women Who Have Made the World A Better Place

Raymond Coutu

Contents

Rigby

A Harcourt Achieve Imprint

www.Rigby.com
1-800-531-5015

S0-BAO-459

Introduction

Have you ever seen something happen that you didn't like? Maybe you saw a friend being bullied on the playground. Maybe you saw an entire city being destroyed by a flood. What did you do? Did you sit back or did you take action?

The following five people did take action. They started **nonprofit** organizations, or groups that help others. Although their goals varied, these people share one thing in common: they cared about making the world a better place.

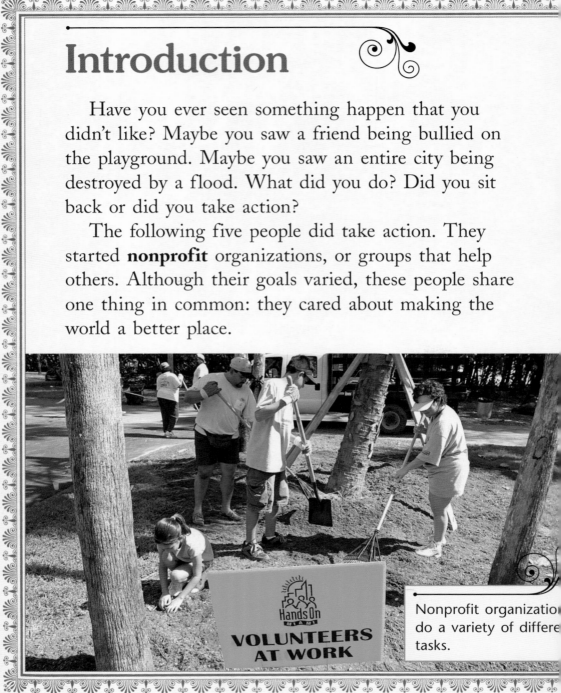

Nonprofit organization do a variety of differe tasks.

What Is a Nonprofit Organization?

A nonprofit organization is a group of people who work together to help others who may not be able to help themselves. These groups do not make money for themselves. Instead, the people that work for these groups raise money that is used to help others.

The money these kids make recycling will go to help others.

Henry Bergh

FOUNDER of

The American Society for
the Prevention of Cruelty
to Animals (ASPCA)

Established 1866

The ASPCA is the oldest animal-protection group
in the United States. The main goals of the group are
to prevent animals from being hurt by humans, to
pass and **enforce** laws that protect animals, and to
take care of animals that have been mistreated and do
not have homes.

The ASPCA was founded
to make sure all animals
have what they need to
survive—including water.

Henry Bergh had wealth, power, and a loving family. So why would this successful man devote his life to improving the lives of animals? The answer is simple—he loved animals. He wanted to change a common belief in the 1800s that animals couldn't feel pain and, therefore, could be treated any way people wanted to treat them.

Henry Bergh

Henry was born in 1813 to a wealthy shipbuilder in New York City. He enjoyed watching ships arrive at the docks that lined the East River. He also enjoyed attending band concerts and visiting the small zoo of a family friend.

As a young man, Henry was given a government position in St. Petersburg, Russia, by President Abraham Lincoln. While living there, Henry saw horrible examples of animals being mistreated. He saw horses harmed for "laziness," cats harmed for meowing, and dogs harmed simply because they didn't have a home. This angered Henry so much that he decided to devote his life to protecting animals.

The ASPCA helps protect stray dogs such as this one from harm.

When Henry returned to New York, he talked to many important people who could help him with his mission. He asked them to sign a document called "A Declaration of the Rights of Animals," which led to the creation of the ASPCA and laws that are meant to stop people from harming animals.

The money to purchase the ASPCA headquarters in New York City was donated by a wealthy fur trapper who at the end of his life regretted having hurt so many animals during his lifetime.

Once these laws were in place, Henry made sure they were enforced. He patrolled the streets of New York, stopping **streetcar drivers** from beating their horses and dogcatchers from killing innocent strays. He stopped events in which people hurt animals for entertainment, such as pigeon shoots, dogfights, and even P. T. Barnum's circus. Henry made surprise visits to places such as **dairies** to make sure animals were being treated well.

Henry's dream to keep animals safe is still alive today. Since the ASPCA was founded, many other animal-protection groups have formed across the country.

Henry Bergh wrote this letter to the president of the New York streetcar line in 1868.

Dear Sir:

*Last night, almost exhausted with **labors** of the day, I saw on the Bowery one of your horses which had fallen from simple overwork. The poor animal was lame . . . and would have died had I not stopped and devoted an hour to its care. When too **fatigued** to do much more, I went home with a heavy heart, saddened more than I can express and, perhaps, to be laughed at for my pains.*

Henry Bergh

Clara Barton

FOUNDER of

The American Red Cross
Established 1881

The American Red Cross is group that helps victims of natural disasters. When hurricanes, tornadoes, wildfires, and earthquakes strike, American Red Cross workers provide food, clothing, and support to people who need them. The symbol of the red cross on the white flag represents **neutrality**.

The American Red Cross also holds many nationwide **blood drives**. In fact, the American Red Cross is the largest supplier of blood to hospitals in the United States.

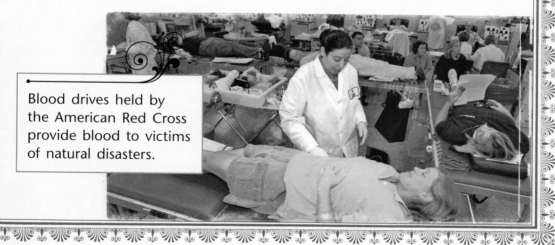

Blood drives held by the American Red Cross provide blood to victims of natural disasters.

9

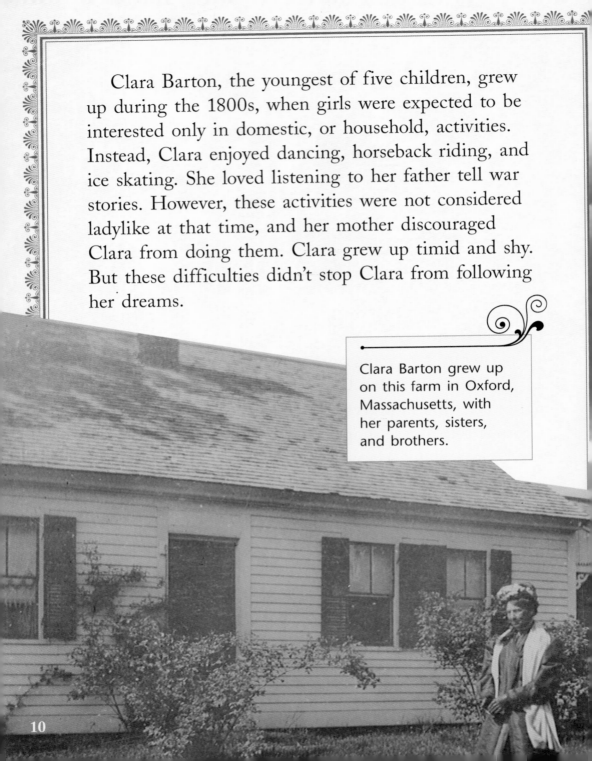

Clara Barton, the youngest of five children, grew up during the 1800s, when girls were expected to be interested only in domestic, or household, activities. Instead, Clara enjoyed dancing, horseback riding, and ice skating. She loved listening to her father tell war stories. However, these activities were not considered ladylike at that time, and her mother discouraged Clara from doing them. Clara grew up timid and shy. But these difficulties didn't stop Clara from following her dreams.

Clara Barton grew up on this farm in Oxford, Massachusetts, with her parents, sisters, and brothers.

When Clara was eleven, her brother David fell from the rafters of the family barn and was seriously injured. Clara helped nurse him back to health over the next two years. While doing so, she realized that helping sick people was meant to be her life's work.

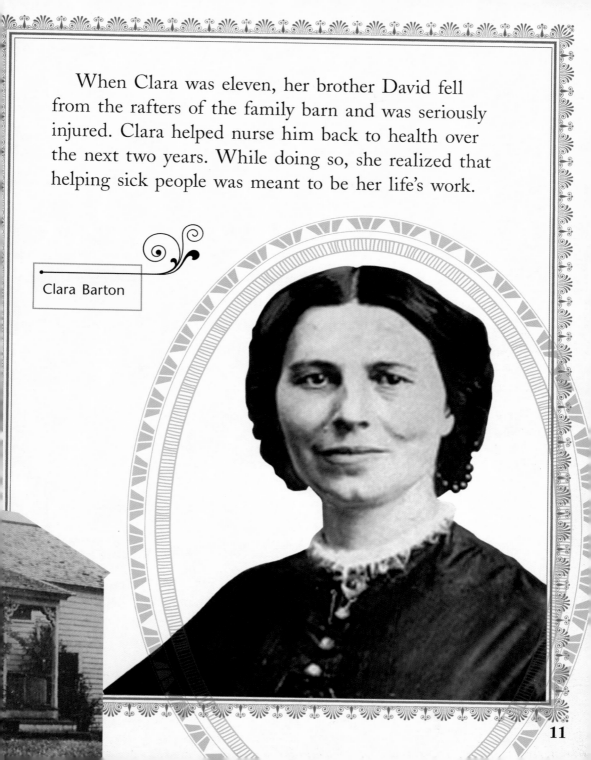

Clara Barton

At the start of the Civil War, after many years of working in Massachusetts and New Jersey as a teacher, Clara took a job in Washington, D.C. While there, she learned about the horrors of war. Food, medicine, blankets, bandages, and crutches were not reaching soldiers who were dying on the battlefields.

Clara decided to gather those supplies and deliver them to the soldiers herself. Getting permission to do this was difficult because at the time, women were not allowed to do such work. Clara was eventually given permission. She saved many lives and found out what had happened to thousands of missing soldiers. She became known as the "angel of the battlefield."

Clara Barton cared for wounded soldiers during the Civil War.

Though the war ended in 1865, Clara continued her mission. She was determined to help as many people as she could. During a trip to Switzerland, Clara learned about the International Red Cross, a group that provided medical services to soldiers in a war, no matter which side the soldiers were fighting on. She was determined to create such an organization in the United States. This organization would not only help soldiers, but it would also help victims of natural disasters, since there were no national **agencies** to do that kind of work. Clara established the American Red Cross in 1881. It continues to carry out Clara's mission to this day.

American Red Cross workers provided food, clothing, and care to people who were injured and left homeless by Hurricane Katrina in 2005.

Franklin D. Roosevelt

Founder of the
March of Dimes
Established 1938

Originally called the National Foundation for **Infantile** Paralysis, the March of Dimes was founded to stop the spread of polio and help people infected by this disease. The goal today for the March of Dimes is to find cures for many health problems that affect babies and children by supporting medical research and educating the public.

Franklin D. Roosevelt

Like Henry Bergh, Franklin D. Roosevelt grew up in a wealthy family. On his father's estate in Hyde Park, New York, Franklin would ride horses, go fishing, and go boating. He was cared for by a governess and taught by a private tutor. Franklin had relatives in important political positions, including his uncle, President Theodore Roosevelt.

As an adult, Franklin's good luck continued. He was popular, smart, and strong-minded. It looked like he would have a successful future in politics. But during a visit to his family's summer cottage, he contracted polio and lost the use of his legs. Franklin was 39 years old, and his life had just changed.

Facts About Polio

- Polio is a disease caused by a virus that can damage the nervous system.

- The virus enters the body through the mouth, usually from unsafe drinking water or dirty silverware.

- People infected with polio often become paralyzed, which means they are unable to move certain body parts.

- A vaccine, or drug, is available to stop the spread polio.

- Since the vaccine's discovery, polio is extremely rare in the U. S. However, it continues to be a problem in other parts of the world.

After many unsuccessful attempts to walk again, Franklin was discouraged. Eventually he learned about a resort in Georgia called Warm Springs. Warm Springs had pools filled with mineral water that, Franklin was convinced, could stop and even reverse paralysis. He met other people with polio there, including many children. In 1926, Franklin bought Warm Springs and turned it into a **rehabilitation** center where polio patients could get medical treatment and emotional support.

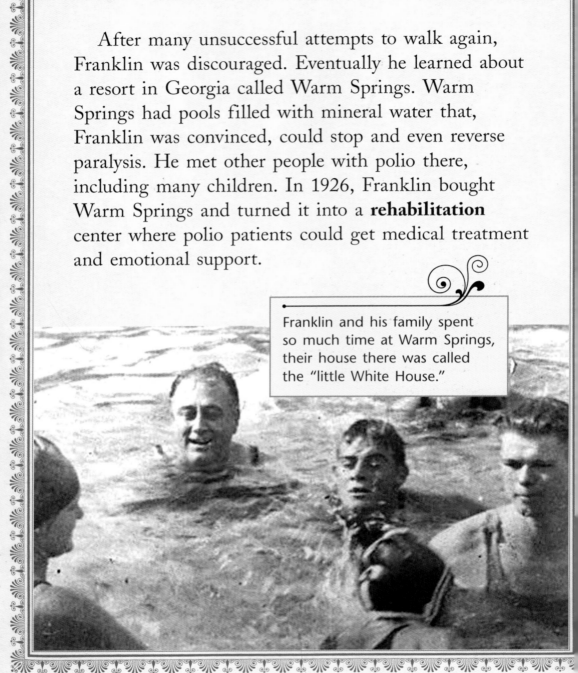

Franklin and his family spent so much time at Warm Springs, their house there was called the "little White House."

Despite his paralysis, Franklin was elected President of the United States in 1932. That was the good news. The bad news was that polio was spreading throughout the world at a frightening rate. The disease had to be stopped. Warm Springs was not enough, so Franklin created the National Foundation for Infantile Paralysis.

Facts About

Franklin's Illness

Because of Franklin's advanced age—39 years old—when he contracted polio, some people think he may have had a different disease. Polio usually affects babies and young children, so some researchers believe that Franklin actually had Guillain-Barré syndrome, a disease that attacks the nervous system.

This is one of the few photographs taken of Franklin in his wheelchair.

The foundation's main purpose was to support medical research that would lead to a cure for polio. Believing that people could solve any problem if they worked together, Franklin asked every American to send dimes directly to the White House. The effort was so successful the foundation's name was eventually changed to the March of Dimes. The campaign earned millions of dollars for research, and finally,

in 1955, Jonas Salk discovered the polio vaccine. Thanks to Franklin and Jonas, polio is no longer a major health problem in the United States.

Many famous people, including movie star Marilyn Monroe, have shown support for the March of Dimes.

Ernesto Nieto

FOUNDER of

The National Hispanic Institute

Established 1979

The National Hispanic Institute helps Hispanic teenagers to prepare for college and to become leaders in their communities. It provides programs for high school and college students that help them develop skills and habits that will allow them to reach their potential while celebrating their culture.

This house is the headquarters for the National Hispanic Institute.

Ernesto Nieto was born in 1940 in Houston, Texas. From a young age he was taught the value of contributing to society. He got his sense of **civic** responsibility from his parents, who were both directors for the Houston City Parks and Recreation Department.

He attended Jefferson Davis High School before receiving an athletic scholarship to the University of Houston. Ernesto then transferred to Southwestern University, where he received a degree in education.

This is the university from which Ernesto graduated.

SOUTHWESTERN
UNIVERSITY
CHARTERED 1840

After Ernesto graduated college, he worked as a teacher and in the government in various state and federal positions. In 1979 he left government business to pursue his dream of creating an institution that would encourage Hispanic students and prepare them for life. The National Hispanic Institute was founded later that year.

Ernesto Nieto

In the past 27 years, the Institute has grown much larger. In 1981 only 90 students were involved in the Institute's Young Leaders Conference. Today the Institute has 8 different leadership programs—including a study abroad program in Mexico—that serve 3,000 to 4,000 students each year.

Facts About

The National Hispanic Institue

- The National Hispanic Institute is located in an old Victorian House in Maxwell, Texas.

- Ninety-five percent of the high school students who participate in a program enroll in college after graduating.

- Ninety percent of the students finish their degrees in five years or less.

Ernesto and his wife, Gloria de Leon, who helped him found the Institute almost 30 years ago, are still very involved in the National Hispanic Institute. In 2001 Ernesto wrote a book about his experiences in creating and running the National Hispanic Institute in its early days. He details the ways in which he had to adapt his idea of the Institute to the reality of his students' lives. Even now, the Institute is growing and changing in an attempt to provide more opportunities to Hispanic students. Ernesto is determined to better the lives of as many students as he possibly can.

Ernesto and his wife, Gloria de Leon

Oprah Winfrey

FOUNDER of

Oprah's Angel Network
Established 1998

Oprah's Angel Network was founded in 1998. The nonprofit organization gives awards and donates aid and money to both individuals and other nonprofit organizations seeking to improve the lives of others. Oprah's Angel Network has a variety of nonprofit groups it supports, including the program Kids Can Free the Children, which raises money to build schools in **rural** areas. Together, the two organizations have built schools in ten different countries, including Mexico, Haiti, and China.

Oprah Winfrey was born in 1954 in Kosciusko, Mississippi. Her family didn't have a lot of money. For the first six years of her life, she was raised by her grandmother on a small farm that didn't even have indoor plumbing. Her grandmother encouraged Oprah to think and taught her to read by the age of three.

From an early age, Oprah was interested in performing. She loved talking and would entertain her grandmother and her friends by reciting passages from the bible.

Oprah spent much of her youth on a farm in Mississippi.

FIRST HOME SITE OF
• Oprah Winfrey •

KOSCIUSKO, MISSISSIPPI

On January 29, 1954, Oprah Winfrey was born in a wood frame house located on this site to Mr. and Mrs. Vernon Winfrey. She resided here as a child before moving to Milwaukee at age six. Within walking distance is the church where she made her first appearance in an Easter recitation.

She grew in the information/entertainment industry to become the world's foremost TV talk show host with a daily audience in the millions. At the same time she never forgot or overlooked her heritage and has been a regular supporter of folks back home as well as a role model to much of America.

When she was six, Oprah went to live with her mother, and at age thirteen, she received a scholarship to a well-known private school. A year later Oprah moved in with her father, who continued to encourage her. He was loving but strict. Oprah has said that she had to submit a book report to him every week. His strictness was effective, however; Oprah won a full scholarship to Tennessee State University, where she decided to study communications.

Oprah got her first reporting job when she was still in high school. By the age of nineteen, she was a reporter for a radio station in Nashville. After she graduated and went to college, she worked as a reporter on a news show.

From a young age, Oprah was determined to work in television.

Oprah wasn't satisfied with being a reporter, but she wanted to stay in television. She accepted a job on a talk show in Baltimore and immediately knew she had found what she wanted to do with her life. In 1983 she took over a morning talk show called *AM Chicago*. Within months, the show was renamed *The Oprah Winfrey Show*, which has, throughout the years, become the most popular talk show in history.

Oprah has been a pioneer for women in television.

In 1997 Oprah did a show in which she encouraged audience members and viewers to send in spare change to help fund scholarships, as well as to donate their time to Habitat to Humanity. This show and the overwhelming response to Oprah's request led her to create Oprah's Angel Network. The foundation has raised over fifty million dollars in aid.

Oprah rose above the disadvantages of her early life to become successful and generous. The world's first African American billionaire, she is determined to use her success and her money to give others the opportunity to live happy, fulfilled lives.

Oprah met hundreds of school children when she visited South Africa in 2002.

Timeline

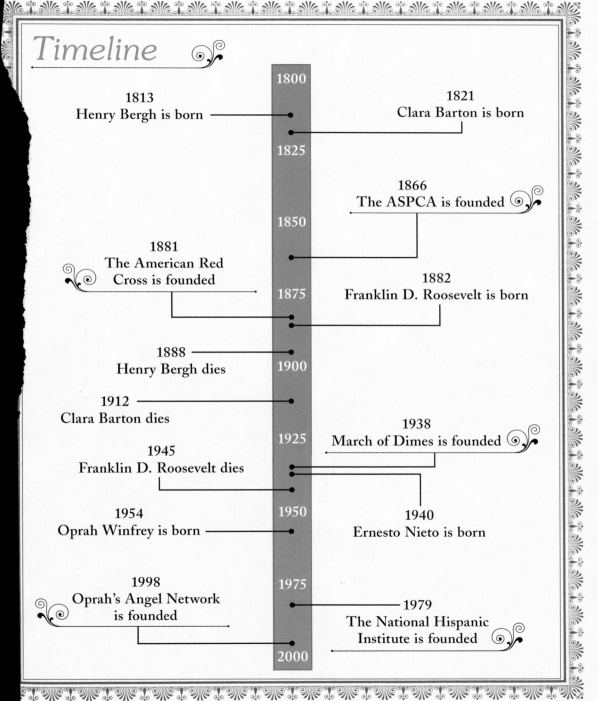

1800

1813
Henry Bergh is born

1821
Clara Barton is born

1825

1866
The ASPCA is founded

1850

1881
The American Red
Cross is founded

1882
Franklin D. Roosevelt is born

1875

1888
Henry Bergh dies

1900

1912
Clara Barton dies

1938
March of Dimes is founded

1925

1945
Franklin D. Roosevelt dies

1950

1954
Oprah Winfrey is born

1940
Ernesto Nieto is born

1998
Oprah's Angel Network
is founded

1975

1979
The National Hispanic
Institute is founded

2000

What Is Important to You?

Protecting animals was important to Henry Bergh. Helping people with injuries and diseases was important to Clara Barton.

What is important to you? How can you make a difference? You can start by choosing something that you are concerned about. Next, learn about that topic by reading books and articles, surfing the Internet, and talking to people who are already involved in helping others. Then find other kids who are interested and talk to local politicians, write newspaper articles, or join walks that raise money to benefit others. Make your voice heard. Become a person of action!

You and your friends can make a difference, too.

Would you like more information about the organizations described in this book? Write or call them.

Facts About Nonprofit Organizations

ASPCA
424 East 92nd Street
New York, NY 10128
(212) 876-7700

The American Red Cross
2025 East Street, NW
Washington, DC 20006
(202) 303-4498

The March of Dimes
1275 Mamaroneck Avenue
White Plains, NY 10605
(914) 949-7166

National Hispanic Institute
P.O. Box 224
Maxwell, TX 78656
(512) 357-6137

Oprah's Angel Network
110 N. Carpenter Street
Chicago, Il 60607

Glossary

agencies organizations

blood drive an event where people give blood to be used for injured or ill people

civic relating to a city

dairies a farm where cows are kept to produce milk and cream

discouraged to become less hopeful

enforce to make sure laws are followed

fatigued tired

infantile affecting babies and children

labor work

neutrality not on one side or the other

nonprofit in business not to make money, but to help other people

rehabilitation to make healthy again

rural relating to the countryside

streetcar drivers people who drove a one-car train that was on tracks and pulled by a horse